BLUE DEER

Four generations of poetry

Colleen A. Slater

Versions of the following poems were previously published
as noted:
Housewife Writers Forum, 1988: 2327 West Sixth,
Accolade from a Daughter, A Question, Childhood Summer
Retreat; 1993: Daddy, Mama; *Priority Parenting*, 1988:
Jamie; *Sandblasted in Point Defiance Promenade*, 1997:
Perseverance; *The Goodnough Gazette*, 1995: Grace, The
Clubhouse Mouse; *The Green Tricycle*. 2000: 2327 West
Sixth, Island Boy; *Key Peninsula News*, 2000: Winter
Morning; *The Peninsula Gateway*, 2002: Ode to Fall; *Voices
From the Key*, 2005: Jo, Lines on a chalkboard at the
YMCA, Notes On A Graduation Picture, Perseverance, Two
of Worlds, Untitled Haiku;

Published by Plicata Press, LLC, Gig Harbor, WA, USA
Cover design and interior art by Sarah Slater, 2011

Library of Congress Cataloging-in-Publication Data

Slater, Colleen A.
Blue Deer: Four Generations of Poetry
ISBN: 978-0-9828205-4-4

Library of Congress Control Number: 2011925135

In memory of
James McCourt O'Hara, my dad,
and
Dennis McCourt O'Hara,
my brother,
for their imagination,
love, and joy in life

ACKNOWLEDGEMENTS

Special thanks to the family members who contributed their poems to this book – son Robert, grandkids Ian, Sarah, and Sheridan. Additional thanks to Sarah, who designed the cover and the interior art.

Thank you to those who encouraged my writing over the years, some of whom are no longer with us: teachers Mildred Campbell, Evelyn Miller, and Dorothy Bouvia-Lusby; my parents, friends, siblings, children, and other relatives; writers in the Gig Harbor Writers' Circle, the Key Peninsula Writers' Guild, and other fellow scribes; faithful readers of my columns and stories in the Key Peninsula News and Peninsula Gateway.

Thank you to Jan Walker for the courage to start Plicata Press, and her encouragement and assistance in getting our books in print.

Most of all, thank you to my "first reader," hubby Frank, for his encouragement, honest critique, and constant love.

INTRODUCTION

Poetry and music have been lifetime companions for me.
Rhyming seemed second nature at a young age.
My first published work was a four-line rhyme in a Sunday
School paper at about age seven. Another rhyme appeared in
the local Vaughn Union High School paper, The Tattler, a few
years later—my cousin Joyce was editor.
One of the poems in this collection began life when I was about
twelve, and has seen a few revisions.
Over the years, rhymes (not all would be considered "poetry")
popped up for various occasions—birthdays, anniversaries,
weddings, graduations, and sympathy cards.
Our annual Christmas letter was rhymed for many years, and
still includes at least a small part in verse.
The idea for this book grew from a wish to share a part of me
with my children and grandchildren. It expanded to include my
father's delightful poem, the inspiration for the book title, and
pieces from son Rob and three grandchildren.
The selections range from playful to serious, sad to joyful.
Perhaps one will touch your heart.

Initials after each selection indicate authors: *CAS* – Colleen
Slater, *RLS* - Robert Slater, *SMMS* – Sheridan Slater, *IRQS* –
Ian Slater, *SS* – Sarah Slater

CONTENTS

CHILDHOOD

NATURE

RELATIONSHIPS

SPECIAL FORMS

OUTSIDE THE BOX

JUST FOR FUN

BIOGRAPHIES

CHILDHOOD

UNTITLED

He's just a boy a wee bit boy
He's scarsely gone on six
But ever since A cun hae min'
He's aye been fu' o' tricks

Dennis is his given name
A'thae ye'd never ken
He ca's hissel maist anything
Wi' mucle hacht 'n fen

Et times he says he's Davy
Tae the wean's high elation
Then he's admiral o' the navy
In his imagination

He thinks nae much o 'awn tae schule
Education fur tae hear
He'd rather dauner up the hill
A chasing bright blue deer

His hauns an' face are seldom clean
As outside roon he'll scatter
'n the only thing that makes him mean
Is the threat o' soap 'n watter

Ne're tired enough tae go tae bed
It's nae fun being there
Bit watch a wee 'n shin yu'll see
Him sleepin' on the flare

He micht no be the brightest boy
Or gifted wae a name
Yet A cunny help bit think some day
He's share tae rise tae fame

'n if he disna, well wha cares
He's fulled some herts wae joy
A often wish he'd never chinge
Bit aye be my wee boy

James McCourt O'Hara
1945

This poem by my dad was untitled. Born and raised in Scotland, a few of his writings used his native dialect.

Dennis, my younger brother, was a cheerful cherub with a vivid imagination. He may well have "seen" bright blue deer daunerin' up the hill.

VIEW FROM A WINDOW SEAT

Chaos in the Heavens
Jagged swords
reflecting in the Bay

Daddy's comforting arm
His soothing voice
crooning gentle melodies of magic
reciting tales of little men
playing bowls in the sky

Strange beauty of that night
struck a response in my soul

CAS

SHELTON, 1940

strawberries
railroad tracks
two big girls
with pigtails
and pleasant faces
peanut butter sandwiches
picnic on the grass

down the hill to town
Daddy in a new sweatshirt
it looked like underwear
I was four
embarrassed

CAS

STRAW HATS
Delano Beach, 1941

Height of fashion
Undreamed extravagance
Straw hats with ribbons and flowers

Sun sparkling on roadside daisies
Breeze catching our voices
swirling them into extinction

Hats snatched by the wind
dance across clovered fields
into oblivion

Retracing the route
scouring the meadows
Tear scalded eyes
grieve lost loves

CAS

THE SPANKING
Darrington, 1942

She called across the street
Come play in the new sprinkler
Wear your swimsuits

Please, Mama, can we get swimsuits?

No, her eyes sad, her voice soft
We don't have money for swimsuits

We watched at the gate
sun hot on our backs
Laughter and squeals
reverberating around us

Come on
I tugged at my brother
My sister followed

The Knick Knack shop had swimsuits
Mama said we could charge them
The lady smiled as she wrote up the slip
We put our clothes in the store bag

Sprays of icy water
Pleasure of friendship
Paradise in the afternoon

Mama cried when she spanked me
Don't you understand?
She closed her bedroom door
My brothers and sisters cried
the little ones in sympathy

Ice surrounded my heart
Salt stung my eyes
Credit is expensive

CAS

7

FIRST GRADE
Darrington, 1942

hopscotch lines
chalked on the sidewalk
boys jostling one another
high school girls pausing to watch
understanding

spaces drawn for third graders
my legs were too short
I practiced on Saturdays

standing in line
waiting for the high school girls
cries of surprise and delight
clapping hands
hugging arms

I understand opening nights

CAS

SAUK RIVER PICNICS

Skipping stones across the water
Sand in our shoes
Icy water to dabble our toes
Bread and butter pickle sandwiches

Mama wore dresses

AGATE BEACH, 1943

Rough plank cookhouse floor
Benches and tables
Aggie's pancakes
Dennis hoped to marry Aggie

Big men with big trucks
Trainmen waving and ringing the bell
Behind the fence
We watched from the big stump

CAS

9

IN TOUCH

I wrote letters before I started school
with fountain pen and smooth paper
to Grandma, aunts and cousins
learning cursive slowly

In second grade, we moved

The teacher needed fat pencils
Thick tablets of soft paper
Printed words

I wrote letters
with my mother's pen
on smooth white paper
Cursive writing
Drawing with thin pencils

Away from Teacher's critical eye

CAS

CHILDHOOD SUMMER RETREAT

Behind the asparagus
shaded by the apple tree
on a blanket
A book for company
I created worlds

CAS

SEASONS OF CHILDHOOD
Vaughn, 1944

FALL

Saturday
Library day
We spent the morning
reading and choosing
After lunch we slid
in sock feet
on freshly waxed floors
Princes and Princesses at a Grand Ball

WINTER

Opening the old trunk
Odor of musk
Delicate ivory fan
Velvet hats, lacy shawls
Faded photographs and letters
Images created in my head
Faraway places and people
I would never know

SPRING

Trillium hunting in the woods
eagerly searching the jewels of Spring
wary of venturing too far
wondering how far to the end of the woods
what was beyond
Handfuls of perfumed flowers
to set in jars and take
to the old neighbors

We didn't know they shouldn't be picked

SUMMER

Building roads under the pine
in the warmth of the early morning sun
Learning to swim with water wings
The bay was not so cold then
Picnics at the beach
Potatoes and cob corn roasted in foil
Banana Jell-O for family gatherings
Anti-i-over the woodshed
Kick the Can at dusk
until we could not see
and friends were called home

Tomorrow a distant future

CAS

HOUSE IN THE DELL

Fragrance of green canopies
Rooms leading into one another
A cat curled up in pleasure

Secrets whispered
as we lay on beds of fern
soft, sweet, fresh each day

Far away
noise of traffic and dogs
muted by feathery curtains

Domain of the young
Did ever ferns grow so high
anywhere else?

CAS

JAMIE

Jamie, Jamie, Jamie
What means that name to me?
I close my eyes and there appears
a face that's dear to see.
Two eyes of blue, a dimple, too,
a cheerful little smile.
Oh boy of mine, remain a boy
for yet a little while.

MICHAEL

There is a child, a wee small tot
who is our pride and joy
Michael is his given name
and he's our second boy
He has a twinkle in his eye
and a mischievous grin
If you but know him for a while
your heart he's sure to win

CAS

CRAYONS FOR MIRANDA

The open box sits on the table, full

The tiny fingers reaching out to find

a treasure chest of colors, none are dull

A color matches one that's in her mind

A line is drawn; ideas start to flow

The picture from her imagination

The order of the box begins to go

A mess will be there when she is all done

Out of the lines and shapes the picture's seen

A smile across my face as I wonder

the places that her little mind has been

There is not one line that is a blunder

Her masterpiece is done, she shows it 'round

The crayons sit forgotten on the ground

SMMS

CAT IN THE WOODSHED

Big and yellow
A camouflage of rust and peeling paint
Heavy tracks immobile
     A place to hide
     A place to dream
Only a shell of what it was
Like my memories

Oily, sticky scents
Sawdust chips and weeds
Damp, mildewy, leather-like seat
Tracks, top and treads, now tables
For coffee cans of cultch
A pile of pieces without a point
Only needed after they've gone to the dump
One man's garbage; another man's gold

It sticks in my mind
     A place of safety
     A place of escape
From where I sit a place of sanity
But in a child's mind I know
Life was just as strange then as now
Still there are spaces of safety and sanity
Only the camouflage has changed

RLS

OUT AND IN

For Ralph G. Slater

You feel the air, the ropes in your hands
You pull your feet in and out, you fly
Higher, racing the others to new heights
     You're out
     You're in
Even when you're out, you're in

You hit the ball back and forth
In the square, out of the square
This is life, your friends
     You're out
     You're in
Even when you're out, you're in

The ball spins round the pole
Back and forth from hand to hand
Tethered, but swinging away
     You're out
     You're in
Even when you're out, you're in

The metal circle spins round and round,
Legs race, feet pound then lift and scream
And fly away from the center, pulled outward
     You're out
     You're in
Even when you're out, you're in

Against the wall, dodge the ball
We jump and fall, success and failure
Are one and the same avoiding, welcoming the hit
    You're out
    You're in
Even when you're out, you're in

An old man ambles by on the street
Kid's voices call names, you're ashamed
You do nothing, not even call the name you know
    Grandfather
    Grampa
Even when you're in, you're out

He wanders on, maybe not even hearing
But you heard, you know, but will you tell?
Keep it in, don't let it out, you're inside out
    You're in
    You're out
Even when you're in, you're out

RLS

UNTITLED

Child

running, jumping

laughing, singing, smiling

swings, slides, trikes, bikes

talking, working, driving

older, aging

Adult

SMMS

DIRECTIONS

A brown cardboard box, heavy
Freed from its colored paper
Rattle of metal, squish of Styrofoam inside
Strip off the strapping tape taking cardboard with it
        Directions. Who needs them?

Pull out some of the parts
Everything fit so nice
Black and red, bolts and wheels,
Braces and handles, big red wagon
        Directions, Daddy? Who needs them?

Radio Flyer, like the one I had
But without the rust and dents
Those will come. So will bruises and scrapes of skin
Put it together. Wheels here, bolts there
        Daddy. Directions. Who needs them?

Fitting together, pretty, perfect
Almost done, boy inside the box. "Look at me."
Hammer red caps on axles, tighten down bolts
What are these parts for, Papa?
        Directions. Damn. Who needs them?

Frustration. Hammer of temptation, inspiration
Hack saw, pliers, one bent hanger, straightened
Pound, saw, bend, finished solid, if not as pretty
It will last till the next generation appears
        Directions? Daddy needs them.

RLS

21

ISLAND BOY

For Shane

Boy of the Island with sparkling eyes
calling the wild deer by name
watching the squirrels store up for winter
thinking that you'd do the same

Alone on your bike along bumpy roads
warrior in helmet you'd ride
Playing Nintendo with bubbling laughter
keeping the pain pushed aside

Talking of somedays when you would be better
the world of Disney you'd see
Hopes and bright dreams of a seven year old
The somedays that never would be

Now you are free as the gulls overhead
free as the wandering deer
You can see many places
and tell us great things

but we
     left behind
          can't yet hear

CAS

NATURE

O MORNING BRIGHT

O morning bright, for thee I mourn
I'm waiting for the coming dawn
I've waited long to see the day
It's growing light as here I lay
The sun is up, the dew is bright
The sky is gray in morning light
Nothing more beautiful have I e'er seen
than trees and grass of shining green
than many birds, each with a song
than distant mountains - For so long
have I been waiting just to see
the rising sun and feel in me
that beauty such as all of this
was made for me, to never miss
to see each day where e'er I go
Someone it seems has told me so
I know not who has told me such
but this I know – just this much
beauty rare as I have seen
should others see and to them mean
as much as just this morn to me
has meant - just as 'twas meant to be

1949
CAS

MORNING/MOURNING

Outside in the cold
Daylight breaks over mountaintops
Pink sky echoes pain

A smile breaks from lips
Long sealed by doubt and sadness
Sunshine breaks through clouds

Crisp dawn air cuts deep
Exposing nerves warm from sleep
Aches of past new days

Pain, like a bird,
Fly away into the clear air
Memory remains

RLS

ARTIST'S POINT – MT BAKER, WASHNGTON

Skeleton spar seeking sky
Above us eagles fly
Settling snow splitting into a crevasse
Silver cerulean solar cell
Culling energy from the air

Rocks worn and round greet me
We step up, step off of the level
The nearby rocks are split and broken
Fractured like many gigantic stone tablets
Waiting for writing

Defiant daisies, flowers of yellow, blue
Ferns clinging to cracks and creases
Half-buried bones of trees snake through stones
Patiently splitting them apart
Furry brown rodents hide in plain sight

Pretty pink flowers fight for soil and energy
Today they get their fill
The blue of the sky is unreal
Broken only by a line of white
The human hubris of our flight

My breath is short
But this air is so preciously pure
I need less of it to live well
I climb, stumbling on loose shale
To the cairn-covered cap of Table Mountain

As we descend birds fly soundless by
Then blackbirds come, chattering
Reprimanding our invasion
Playing on the air currents
Enjoying the day and its glory

Artist's point, a fitting name
Who can see this beauty,
See it and not be touched,
Not be happy to be alive today,
To be a witness to this grandeur?

RLS

SUNSET QUILT

The sunset is like a quilt

its many colors shine

You can see them 'til dark

and then you need a light.

Red, pink, purple, orange, and yellow

the colors patch together

like a quilt on a bed before night.

SMMS

PERSEVERANCE

Steep bank bereft of green
Twisted root of Madrona exposed
A lone tiger lily makes an exclamation point
A signal to the world passing by
that the impossible can be accomplished

*This original poem was cut to 100
characters and spaces to submit to
the Poetry on the Promenade contest,
sponsored by Puget Sound Poetry
Connection and Metropolitan Park
District of Tacoma. One of 15 winning
entries, it was sandblasted into the
Point Defiance Promenade in 1997
with an artist's interpretation*

Steep bank bereft of green
Twisted Madrona root exposed
A tiger lily makes an exclamation point

CAS

SUMMER SCENE

Graceful dancing damsel

dressed in creamy lace

dipping, gliding, swaying

forever in her place

Rooted where she's growing

still she'll twist and sway

with every passing wind breath

The Lady Ocean Spray

(Ocean Spray -- *Holodiscus discolor* -- is a deciduous shrub
native to Western Washington, Oregon and British
Columbia.
Creamy white at peak of bloom, it fades to brown)

CAS

30

WEATHER

I
face the cold door
and the wind and the rain
The door jumps out of my cold hands
slams into the wall
Wind-whipped water washes over me
stinging my eyes
I run across the plaza
My room is shelter
I race to its warmth
shake off, coat on chair
sink into its softness, relieved
I reach for my coffee
hot, chocolaty, sugary heat
And realize
I left it behind
I face the cold door and the wind and the rain again

RLS

31

STANZAS IN A STORM

Wind rattles through the windows
Rumbles through the floorboards
Odd sounds, creaking, a tree limbs scrapes
Fingernails on a chalkboard

The lights flicker
The sounds grow and fall
Crescendo, decrescendo
Rising, falling, rising

Scrape, claw
Rumbleshake
Flash, the sound builds
Trembling

The lights flash and go out
The wind whistles out and in
Slowing now, finally more gentle
Then calm quietness returns

After a time the lights return
I switch them off and slip back into bed
I wrap myself up in you like a blanket and fade into sleep
The storm has passed.

RLS

ODE TO FALL

Last of September, heralded by
falling of leaves multi-hued
Trees rustle gently, whisp'ring goodbye
Summer has now been subdued
Gone is the brilliance of sunshine so warm
Gone are the birds chirping gaily each morn
Forgotten as Autumn comes scurrying in
fortelling the coldness of wintry wind
Goodbye to the summer, farewell to it all
September is fading
Let's welcome the Fall

CAS

WINTER SCENE

Ice and snow, frozen in time
Crystal beauty reflecting starshine
Untrammeled perfection
Soundless night
Motionless
Cold as
Eternity

CAS

MY WINDOWS NEED WASHING

The birds are full of music
Sunlight beckons
after days of rain

I must go admire the trilliums
Johnny-jump-ups
young green oxalis

Scatters of color
against evergreens and barren earth
Fresh canvasses heralding a new season

Geese overhead
proclaiming Spring
Time to move on to new adventures

The windows will be there tomorrow

CAS

2327 WEST SIXTH

Early morning sunrise
Pastel swatches
streak the sky
Fogbank swaddles
the city below

Panorama of sky and sea
Flashing lighthouse light
Ballet of seagulls
Smoke banners
Dancing leaves

Chipmunks gossip in crabapple
Finches pirouette through alders
Pigeons weight elderberries

I turn from the window
with hidden tears
Tomorrow we move

CAS

RAINBOW

Over here the sun is shining
Look there how raindrops fall
Feel the sun warm your back
Gaze through the droplets

Discover a rainbow

CAS

RELATIONSHIPS

MAMA

Reading
Lying on a blanket on the grass
Wearing an old high school gymsuit
We stay away, allowing her quiet time
Her hair smooth
shiny black
all in place
The shapeless gymsuit
looks good on her
Her face
absorbed in the book
smoothed out and pleasant
For a time she is not
mother of five
breadwinner for seven
tired but patient
She is beautiful
She is free

DADDY

Tall and slim
cigarette in hand
squinting at the sun
beneath his hat brim
an easy slouch
twinkling eyes
ready smile
a story or song
even a quick dance
for the young ones
but always an audience
notepad stuffed in a pocket
blue fountain pen
words, phrases,
names and events
spiral notebooks with
poems, story beginnings,
notes for letters back home
Making connections

CAS

Teller of Tales

Not much of a father, you weren't the stayin' kind
You woulda been a good one if you'd a taken the time
You had six children, one of them had me
I'm just a branch on your family tree
I'm a chip off your block, though I settled down
Got your thirst for knowledge and an ear for a sound
Read some of your stories, heard some second hand
I know things didn't turn out quite the way that you planned

Chorus
You were a dreamer of dreams,
Though most didn't come true
You were a searcher for freedom
Probably shoulda sang the blues
You were a teller of tales
Now I'm tellin' yours, too
Wish I'd known you, Scotty
But that wish won't come true

You went from town to town, didn't hold down a job
Sometimes took your family, but you went where you were
called
You died when I was two, a stormy night in '69
The end of a life, lived out of its time
Your restless ways would've served you best
If you'd come from Scotland out to the old west
But in 1931, to this country you came
There weren't enough jobs and the Wild West was tame
Chorus

29 Dec 1992
For my grandfather, James "Scotty" McCourt O'Hara.
Inspired by a Radney Foster song (or two).

RLS

HANDS

Looking at my hands in the light
I realize they're not my hands alone
There are others who have shared their joy and pain
They are the hands of my father
And his father before him
And I know some day my sons' will look the same

These hands are good hands
Through time they've served us well
They've picked up scars and picked up children, too
Dried and cracked and sometimes bruised
If they could talk they'd tell you tales
Of sad and happy times they've pulled us through

RLS

TEENANGST POETRY

Fire

As I stare into the fire
The flames of my desire
Burn higher as I dream of what may be

The glow of the coals
Reflects the millions of souls
Whose dreams within the fire I see

The heat comes forth
Like life from the hearth
As it has for so many centuries

As the embers crack
My mind goes back
To so many childhood memories

Coming in from the cold
To the fire so bold
To sit and gaze into the sparks within

The fire reveals us
Yet cloaks and conceals us
From the extremities of sainthood and sin

Our loves and our needs
Show in the words and deeds
That show our fascination for the fire

The love I feel for you
Barely controlled it's true
Lights the sky up with passion burning higher

I stare into the flames
Trying to forget your name
But its an internal, eternal fire which burns

A fire you can't quench
With any water that you drench
For as long as this old world beneath us turns

RLS

FATHER'S FATHER, FATHER'S MOM

Father's Father, Father's Mom
Up they get in early dawn
Clip the roses, mow the lawn
Young in spirit, full of wisdom

Daddy's Daddy, Daddy's Mama
Never rushed, but never late
At my house two hours 'till eight
Playing cards, but never keeping data

Papa's Papa, Papa's Mum
Bakes the brownies, cooks the cake
Chocolate, vanilla, strawberry quake
Wait your turn, there's enough for all to have
some

Grandpa, Grandma, Daddy's Parents
Forever cherishing these moments.

SS

DEMISE OF A MARRIAGE

To love, honor and cherish
You promised
Forsaking all others
Forever

You lied

LINES ON A CHALKBOARD AT THE YMCA

You said we would play games
Just have fun
We wouldn't have to hold hands

You said

CAS

COFFEE GIRL

Your free coffee? Sure. What would you like?
Frenchvanillalattetall.
I'll have to charge you for the flavor. Smile.
Twinkling eyes.
32 cents.
Keep the change.
Thanks. Real smile from her teeth to her eyes.
Looking for a book, searching the stacks, no luck.
I see her again through the bookshelf.
Humming to herself.
Coffee up. Here you go. Have a nice day.
Thanks. You too.
Still searching the stacks.
Still no luck.
Leaving the store, she's getting in a car,
Battered, primered, puttering blue smoke,
Boyfriend, leather jacket, gray hoody, reeks
attitude,
Like the cigarette dangling out the window.
Ashes floating down to the pavement.
She slams the door.
Twinkle gone. Coffee in one hand, cig in other,
Sits close to the door.
He's not smiling either. You're late!
I was working.
Back to their room to be alone together.

RLS

46

UNTITLED TO YOU

In some ways it's easier when you're gone
Dancing, playing guitar, singing, swimming, drawing,
performing
I imagine you happy
Though my brain says it cannot always be

When you are here
I wonder how long you will stay
And the day you leave
My love is expressed as anger and frustration

Then you are gone
The house is quieter
The other children look for you to come in the door
Or walk out of the door to your rooms

There is a part of me gone
That I think about when I can't sleep
That I notice in the quiet
That I hurt less when nothing reminds me

But something always does
One of the little ones
Laughs or moves like you
And it floods back

Just like now, a thought, something intellectual
Dances, plays, sings, swims, draws, transforms
Into something else
A feeling of missing, of waiting, of tears

In some ways it's easier when you're gone
But mostly it's easier when you're here

RLS

HOW COULD YOU HAVE DOUBTED?

You called   I came
You asked   I answered
You hurt   I comforted

But sometimes when you spoke
you thought I didn't listen
Sometimes when you reached
you thought I wasn't there

Still, I hadn't moved

It was you who stepped back
You who didn't speak
You who wouldn't ask
You who chose another way
A way I could not see
A way I could not follow

How could you have doubted?

CAS

A FEATHER FOUND

I found a feather, long and gently curved,
Golden brown so fine,
A tool for flight

A feather to tickle your fancy,
Shall I tease your tender toes,
Touch your tips with this feather's brush?

I found a feather, long and gently curved,
Golden brown so fine,
A tool for flight,
Turned to a tool for joy and laughter

A quill pen to tease your thoughts,
To create tantalizing pictures in your mind,
Words whispered into reality

I found a feather, long and gently curved,
Golden brown so fine,
A tool for flight,
Turned to a tool for flights of fantasy

RLS

IN MEMORY OF JO

Messages fly, people connect
Strangers now acquaintances, even friends
Her wide circle becomes closer
weaving threads in her name

She would laugh with joy
to see what she created

She loved so much and so many
People
Animals
Stories
Music
Myth
Nature

One is reminded of her at every turn
Jo would like that …
I remember when Jo …
Like her story of …
I must tell Jo …

One who has lived and loved
laughed and wept and shared
depths and heights
Is never gone
but forever with us

CAS

JO

The waters are cold and gray now
One day the loons will come back
to give their plaintive call
and she will return
to be one with them in spirit

A reminder of her presence
among us

CAS

DARE TO LOVE

Dare to love
Dare to be happy
Dare to be faithful and true
Ignore the rumors, the rumblings of sorrow
Dare to love many, not few
Dare to face life
Rejoice in your living
Find beauty for which your soul yearns
Dare to be loving, kind and good hearted
And you shall be loved in return

1949

CAS

A QUESTION

How is it he comes home to me?
No stately beauty, I
No raven hair, no figure Greek,
no soft bewitching sigh
What draws him here I cannot tell
nor is this often queried
for I'm the one to whom he comes
and I'm the one he married.

.

AWAKENING

Wake me with a kiss, a tender kiss
Touch me with your hands, your gentle hands
When at last my eyes are open
and I see your loving smile
I know that here beside you
is my heaven

CAS

COME WALK WITH ME

Come walk with me and we will go
to a quiet place where flowers grow
Where we can walk without a word
and wait for nature to be heard

Come walk with me through the silent wood
where thoughts can pass and be understood
We'll stop awhile our minds to share
and find a peace as we go from there

Come walk with me as we go through life
and I'll do my best as a loving wife
Give me your hand each even'tide
and we'll go together side by side

CAS

A LOVE POEM

When I was a little girl, I never had a doubt
I knew that when I grew a bit, it would all turn out
One day a shining knight would ride upon a gallant steed
Strong of arm and true of heart, doer of valiant deed
I knew not how or where or when,
but I was a firm believer then
Later on I worried some if it would come about
For I was shy and insecure and short and rather stout
Not tall and willowy as I dreamed, not beautiful with poise
Would I always wait and hope and never know love's joys?
Yet suitors came, but went on by
and in despair I'd weep and sigh
Then one day you came along,
true of heart and brave and strong
In my heart I knew at last
my youthful dream was far from past
Your loving eyes seemed to see
deep down inside a different me
You cared so I could grow into the woman you now know
Even when I don't say it right
My love, you are my shining knight

CAS

ACCOLADE FROM A DAUGHTER

My mom's a professional writer
she said to her friend
pride in her voice
awe in their eyes
as they turn to me

Not yet, I object
Nothing is published

She writes neat stories
and poems
she said

They return to their homework
I leave the room
hiding pleasure and surprise

Admiration unsolicited
a bond gently forged
She is fifteen
not given to praise

CAS

UNFOLDING OF A ROSE

As a rose unfolds from bud to bloom
releasing its fragrance as it goes
Its beauty enlarges, expands, exposes
That's the way our loving grows
We met, our petals tightly wrapped
needing warmth and light to show
the loveliness deep within
The gift of love we've come to know

CAS

A MOMENT

What is a moment when it's gone?
I felt my shirtsleeve,
Found it damp
And wondered why

Then it came to me
You and the water spraying and me
Running, holding hands
Disappointment at staying dry

As the memory passes my mind
I wonder out loud
"Did it really happen?"
It seems a dream

But I recall the feeling
And can picture the place
With you and the sunlight and me
But even now it fades

Making its inevitable change
From moments to memories
An endless progression
What is a moment when it's gone?

RLS

WOMAN IN THE MOON

Domestic violence is a factor in her escape
Blasting off to ports unknown
Out of the atmosphere and on her way home

Flagrant schemes to keep her Earthbound
A different interpretation of the circumstances
Ignoring responsibilities she took off for the sky
Hoping there to find some answers

Remarkable restraint, she left him still alive
Cradling his pain and stewing in his anger
He can't afford to face his blame
Along that path lies danger

But she wins the fight by being gone
Away off in the stratosphere and stars
Will she ever land?
Come down from the constellations
Or will she remain as a star to guide others?

RLS

NOTE ON A GRADUATION PICTURE

Save a smile for me
you wrote
I loved you then
We went separate ways
I dreamed
but our time was past
the distance too great
to be bridged
with a gentle
never spoken
affection

Perhaps you don't need it now
but a smile is there for you
Waiting

CAS

AT THE MAIL BOX

First class mail on top
The mail lady knows
What's important

I eye the pile
with a quickening heart
Oblivious to traffic
roaring by
ruffling my hair
like leaves on the trees

Fingers scrabble
Coming to business letters
Too soon
Going back slowly

Gathering clouds
Raindrops spatter on pavement
There is no letter from you

CAS

20 QUESTIONS FOR A FRIEND

For Wayne

Are you an Aquarius?
Is this our age?
Where did you come from?
Why did I feel an immediate bond?
Where have you been these years?
      These centuries?
What does *Anam Cara* mean?
Do you really have the passion you seem to?
Where does your art come from?
Does music sooth your savage soul?
Are you destined to wander?
      Through lands and lives?
Are you a teacher?
      Or simply an inspiration?
Are all your stories true?
When will I see you again?
Will the friendship remain?
How many lives have we traversed
      Awaiting this meeting?
Will we meet again in the next?
Does this happen somewhere,
To someone everyday?

RLS

AN AFTERNOON WITH PABLO NERUDA

Spent I this day lost in a dream of words, of rivers and laughter.
Lost I my way in their beauty,
Two tongues, one well I know and the other more a beloved
stranger,
Known in my heart, yet less known in my head

You helped me to lose my way amongst the river stones
Traced by phrases of love and longing, death and loneliness

I searched for phrases to make myself known to you
A hint of a smile to bring to your eyes
The caress of a word in your ears

Yet, the poet whose words made me weep,
Had no words that seemed fit to fill the empty page you now see
littered with lines

So with his phrases and rhythms,
   Con sus ritmos y frases,
His visions and landscapes of love
   Sus vistas y paises del amor
I have left these words on the shore of your sea
   Estas palabras me ha dejado en su orilla del mar

RLS

UNTITLED

Where you have never traveled, may I take you
my eyes are only silent to the blind
the frail gesture of my wings enclose you,
Do not touch because they too will come undone

Though you are closed, my gentle feathers
as sun lighting on your petals, barely tingle
yet you open as if the light calls you
to unfold the pages of your flower

Yet like a book with a terrible turn, suddenly,
you close. Slamming an epilogue to the plot.
Autumn turns cold, falling into winter as he grasps
his snow white hair swept by the wind

The wind of the world wraps my wings around me
as their fragility is tested: their soft texture torn
compelling you with their countries of color,
breathing the sky's breath of potent rendering death

My wings close as my eyes open, understanding you
as I stand newly naked, nevermore to fly open to the sky
My eyes are dark and deep, but lightening
through your rose-coloured glass half full of rain

RLS

64

REQUEST

Don't bury me in white, for pure I never was
I loved and gave but took and hurt
often without intention
At times without regrets

Black is not my color – I loved life more than that
sunsets and butterflies
cascading waterfalls
music and dancing
people and parties
rippling streams

Remember me as caring, think of me as true
When my time has come
lay me soft
in palest blue

CAS

DIAMOND ME

I

am not

many faced,

but multifaceted.

One for everyone. One

for each one. I am hard when

pushed, my edge can cut, can scar

Yet hit me on a fault I may split to my

core. If you look into my eye, you may see

beauty, but also flaws in my crystalline clarity.

But do I care at all? Is my cut so ideal? Can you see

yourself in me? Can you see me in yourself? If my cut is

poor I will lose your light. Not a princess even without prints

Am I a marquise, a radiant or heart? What rating or grade

may I be given? My edges may cut your glass, marring

the surface of your face with lines bent downward,

yet in your glass I am mirrored with my own

lines and divisions. What colors will you

show? A blue of sadness, and yet lit

by the sun? A gold light shines

from within? Or the redness

of desire, sun fire? Tell

me what I see. Do

you see me

in you

?

RLS

66

SPECIAL FORMS

SONNETS

To Love
To love and those beings worthy of love,
I honor thy lives wherein kindness lurks;
In a child where lies the peace of a dove
A reminder of the fruits of our works.
So if life is for the living, then live,
With a heart full of hope and happiness;
And if love is for the giving, then give,
Till you find all the love with which you are bless'd.
If someone had all the time in the world
Then all who are worth loving could be loved.
We could bloom as an oyster is pearled
And live our lives with the peace of the dove.
        I spread this plea on the winds high above
        To love and those beings worthy of love.

Love In Silent Acclaim
How can we know if the feelings we feel
Will be returned with the same joy to us,
The love between us we sense could be real
If our hearts would just open and trust.
Our greatest fears lie in the chance of loss
Of our friendship in exchange for more.
That our hearts alone can't survive the cost
To sacrifice with eyes from which tears pour.
Love lies in silent acclaim still asking:
How can one tell if love will be returned?
Can one tell a heart from which love will ring;
And the giver blessed or the giver spurned?
        One can't tell which, so we take love's chance
        To bare our souls in this our earthly dance.

Kissed As Reality Anoints

Kissed, as reality anoints her
With the warmth of the sun on her face
Her dark eyes flash as she meets my gaze
I know this I wish to remember
As her dark lips curl into a grin
The glint in her eyes tells me this
That this day will be bless'd with her kiss
Oh, lucky day to kissed from within
For each day that I see her is fine
And the days she is gone are quite dull
As this room without her can't be full
And with her life, my life entwines
      Though this time we have draws to an end
      In my mind she'll return here again

Jewel Of Days Insatiable End

Oh, jewel of days insatiable end,
Why do you tempt me with your heaven's fire?
Why do I, to your sunlight, wish to bend,
And to your improbable love aspire?
Is it because only love keeps us young?
At least a semblance of youth it imparts;
For life must be lived as songs must be sung
Ever repeating the whims of our hearts;
Though likely you'll never know of my love,
And by sunrise it may fade from these eyes;
This night might remain if the stars up above
Will shine down upon us undisguised.
      If this poetry never reaches your ear
      I'll know in my heart that love awaits here.

Love You'll Not Doubt In Eternity

Love, you'll not doubt in eternity
That the love I have for you is real;
It will lie here quiet and patiently
Till the time when it's able to feel;
Don't think that this love's only physical,
It comes from my heart as well as my head;
Outside I appear somewhat cynical,
But in my eyes the truth can be read;
Though this love may remain unrequited,
Please do not regret what we have shared;
Let it stay in your heart well remembered
Always knowing throughout time I've cared;
  Please stay in touch wherever you go
  For a love that's been kindled should grow.

A Memory Binds Every Rhyme

A memory binds every rhyme
And love makes the syllables sing
A verse is a moment in time
A Remembrance for paupers and kings
At this moment you are my muse
Inspiring the words to come forth
When I look in your eyes so amused
My heart makes my mind change its course
Your smile makes me wax poetic
The rhymes stumble free from my mouth
Your voice adds a tune to the music
While your eyes make my heart beat out loud
  If rhymes only memories be
  Come now make music with me

Time Reveals Ev'ry Varied Avenue

Time reveals ev'ry varied avenue
That blessed fate might suggest as our course
When I met you I felt I had known you
As the waters that run know their source
Under raindrops we sat in the courtyard
Under sunshine we lay on the lawn
Sweet music and sound rained down on us
The touch of your voice kept me warm
As a brother I offer you water
As a writer I offer you dreams
May we always share water together
As the current carries us down life's streams
    Through the eddies and tides, the calms and the
    storms
    May the touch of my life your heart warm

What Plays But Human Truth

What plays but human truth on the stage?
Or that, our goal, seems to be.
How to capture a moment of lovely rage
As it escapes from this plane of being.
Then to replay, to reveal this gracious gift
Again and again with life enthralled;
To create wet fire out of time's sifted sands,
To break through the crust 'neath we've stalled.
When success breeds response from the crowds we adore,
Then strong imagination takes hold.
Actors can feel the emotions that haunt the stage
And for that true souls are sold.
    So join in our quest for its great reward
    Is to share in this moment unmarred.

Here I stand no tricks but my tongue
Let the language leave my lips well
If I with feigning voice had sung
Let the truth of the words not tell
Yet give me God's own irony
And tempt me not with your geld
Let me hear the poet's symphony
Spilling forth as magic beheld
No dancing or wooing for me
As the groundlings howls aren't my goal
Rather a hint of a smile to see
For that warmth is raised in my soul
    So give me your hands hard or softly
    If these words have touched you low or lofty

RLS

HAIKU

Gnarled hands filled with love
Deftly, gently train the boughs
Forever Bonsai

Twisted Madrone root
Tiger Lily clings to bank
True perseverance

Golden leaves carpet earth
The dying season is here
Gary left today

CAS

Mars, bright in the sky
Unexplained flashes, fades
Are they coming here?

Sand slips and gives way
Searing my skin, sinking cool
My toes find solace

Sandpaper hair stage
Raindrops penetrate my brain
Where is my hat now?

Sleepy eyelids droop
The coldness keeps us awake
Longing for warm beds

Summer loses heat
Autumn falls away from him
The coolness begins

Pens scrape on parchment
Symbols slip soundlessly past
Signifying like snakes

Metallic tinkling
Melodic voices echo
Calmness is found here

Fecund air ferments
On cool winds running from
Sunshine's searing heat

Rumble of life
Currents of machines
Surging through soil

Old grassy roads
Suffer natures insistent
Insinuating force

Dust motes twinkle
Dancing, swirling around
Chasing, never touching

Dust motes twinkle
Dancing, chasing, never touching
Until they fall

RLS

TANKA

Miranda

A beauty born of us
She lays sleeping, snoring soft
A night owl, she wakes
Bright-eyed in the dark
Seeking comfort, a warm chest

Internment

Look forward peoples
Of the race of humankind
To a future where
All are created equal
But forget not past lessons

9/11

One morning I woke
All the world turned upside down
We are again part
Of the world we looked down on
Welcome back, America

RLS

QUATRAIN

Winter Morning
In creeps morning light
as sleep tiptoes away
Neighbors' rooftops sparkle white
Jack Frost's had his say.

Season's Scene
Fragrance of cinnamon and fir
Candles glowing bright
Kitten purrs on hearth
A Merry Christmas sight

Rainbow
A day of trials
Rainbow paints the sky
Sun reflects through raindrops
A smile through tears

Sunset
Colors etched across the sky
reflected in the bay
Birds know evening's nigh
Softly ends the day

CAS

OUTSIDE THE BOX

I AM

I am a cello shown off, music flowing from its strings

I am a book, consumed even as I'm giving myself for
others' knowledge and entertainment.

I am a movie, projected onto a screen for people to laugh,
scream, cry, or gawk at.

I am a pencil, gripped until a cramp appears.

I am a Frisbee, thrown and caught again, and again.

I am a story, flowing from a zooming pencil, available for
others' consuming.

I am an ear, perked up intently as music flows into it, and
fingers, placed down on all the right notes.

I am a grade, rising and falling as time goes on, but I try to never
go lower than I am.

I am a controller in an overflowing room, used until the two best
friends' hands cramp.

I am a textbook devoured, other times I'm a teacher heard. Sometimes,
I'm just not there.

I am water cut through.

I am a plastic pellet flying through the air as friends play.

I am an advanced math class. Full of students, and yet, sometimes
they gain no knowledge.

I will be a famous symphony, the philharmonic. All performers
earning a living from only that.

IRQS

78

UNTITLED

I then saw peace clearly.

She was slim and strong.

She turned and gently walked forward.

I saw her rainbow of colors inside,

heard her soft whisper,

then I felt at peace inside.

SMMS

UNTITLED

They continue to search,
their stomachs lurch,
you're lying on the ground.

The trees are crying,
leaves are dying,
falling to the ground.

Fall is dreary,
the world is weary,
there's no joy to be found.

The snow is coming,
birds aren't humming,
there's barely any sound.

It's all so gloomy
with winter looming,
trees with frost are crowned.

It's getting colder,
we're growing older,
there's no turning 'round.

Snow starts falling,
voices are calling,
you can hear them, they surround.

You start to weep,
then drift to sleep,
you never will be found.

They continue to search,
their stomachs lurch,
you're lying on the ground.

The snow is slowing,
the search is growing,
you soon appear a mound.

The earth's unthawing,
the cold stops gnawing,
you soon will join the ground.

The birds are flying,
the sky is crying,
new growth will soon be found.

Please don't cry
you're in the sky.
By angels you've been found.

With a wreath of flowers
from Earth's great bowers
Soon you will be crowned.

SMMS

DREAMS

Trust to your dreams, dream nobly
Hold fast to your dreams, dream boldly
Send your dreams awinging up
until they reach the sun
Work and strive toward your dreams
Until you know you've won
Keep your vision high
Keep your eye on beauty
on brightness and perfection
and keep your eye on duty
For this is Work! Wisdom! Action! Life!
And this is God.

1949

CAS

DEATH OF THE MAPLE

The mighty maple is no more
It fell to earth with trembling roar
The giant free of disease at last
its golden leaves forever past
No more will it shelter birds of the air
No more will the path be shaded there
The woodsman measures and cuts on the hill
Fuel to warm in winter's chill

CAS

BALANCE DUE

Cryptic phrases scratched on scraps
Written on recycled paper
The back of a bill
Your Statement
Previous balance
Consumption history
Past due date like the milk in my fridge

Random words on napkins or sticky notes
Torn off corners of homework
Backs of business cards
A coffee card with 9 of 10 punches
For a place you used to sit and write
Or stare at the people walking by
Before the place went out of business
For letting too many people sit and write
Or stare or read other writer's rhymes

Other bad habits like losing keys
Losing those slips of paper with cryptic lines
Writing lines of prose passed off as poetry by
Cutting the sentences in
strange, awkward
Places
Implying there is meaning in those choices

Found in a pile, an envelope with a window
"Thorndike's Folly" – "Pas de Duex"
Impetus long lost
It's Greek to me
Or Latin or French

Someday I'll remember I tell myself
As I place it in the folder
With other foreign phrases,
Unfinished lines and lies

Please return stub with your payment and your stilted poetry

RLS

LEAVING L.A.

A city of a million stars
Every light is for someone
Airstream off the engine fin
Visible in perfect curves
Power surging forward
Contained violence
A leap of faith
Unmitigated human hubris
The right to soar?
Who are we? Who am I?
Away from the lights
Out to sea we bank and turn
Back over dry land, lights below
Golden cul-de-sacs, like Christmas decorations
The horizon's jagged edge echoes the ragged coastline
Climbing above it all
Chasing a sunset
A rainbow of sky from the sea on upward
Subtle stripes from brown to crimson to orange
A line of yellow to green to blue
Blue denim, like faded Levis
Gradually returning to their original blue-black indigo
With Jupiter, a diamond centerpiece of searing white fire
In this prismatic sky
We soar on, another plane, momentarily a star,
flies past
Tempting the universe
Red lights flash under iron wings
Reflecting off her engines
Why she for ships and planes?

My eyes return to the portal again and again and again
Each time I wonder if I alone can see it in this light
"I'm the closest to heaven that I'll ever be"
Iris in the sky
Fire, a brighter, bloodier red gash in the distance
Slashed into the curtain of orange sky near the horizon
Again my eyes return to the sky, the planet,
The other stars begin to poke through the blue velvet curtain
I give up a little of my soul
And get so much back from the beauty
The beauty that surrounds me
I remember to breathe deep
Sucking the colors into my lungs
And the vision into the memory of my soul
I know it won't all stick
But I find a piece of peace
Fleeting, ungraspable, ethereal peace
Who else sees this sky?
I would I could have shared it with you

RLS

IN THE MIND OF A BLACK-WINGED BIRD

I am a black bird flying, floating
The currents lift me up
I carve wind with my wings
My companions are close
We chatter
But only when we think we're alone
Below
The rush of water calls
Amplified by the cliff walls
Others are near
They too chatter and call
They care not if they are alone
They skitter down piles of rocks
Slipping in the bright snow
Their colors set them apart
Colors nature never knew
       They come
       They climb
       They scramble
       They fall
Eating they are quieter
Their young too want food
Yet some chatter like our young

As the sun reaches its height they are gone
Redder now, touched
    By the sun
    By the air
    By the energy of the outdoors
They leave in shiny metal boxes
The scent of their burnt offerings linger
As does the stench of the metal boxes
Trying to keep their wheels on the mountain
Why don't they release their smoking brakes and fly?
    Fly like us
    Free
Carried on the currents of the air
But alas their wings are too small and weak
They will only fly in their dreams

RLS

THE WANDERER

I've walked the richest castle paths
I've smelled the rotting plum
No matter where I've lain my head
I'm gone when daylight comes

I've seen some mighty storms and floods
I've watched the sunset glow
but I must always move along
just like the winds that blow

I've heard the geese fly overhead
I've seen the wild deer run
and when the night has passed away
I'm off to meet the sun

I've walked the crowded city streets
I've sniffed the new mown hay
There's always something new to see
with every dawning day

I've fought the wars and felt their pain
in many a different land
I've asked my God if time will be
when peace will come to man

I've heard a new born baby cry
I've seen the old ones go
I've pondered love and life and death
Some things I'll never know

I've worshiped in cathedrals
and in the open air
I've walked in dust and mud and sand
and found that people care

CAS

STEPS

A scent of fear, of
clarity is playing on air currents,
six steps of brick, worn down by centuries of
feet. I climb a pavilion. In the past, flags flying. Now
empty. Hollow. Only ghosts. More steps: twelve. The sun is near the
horizon. A soft red glow permeates the clouds. I hear a sound. Spinning I spy
a dog, scraggly, skinny,
scared. I whistle, and he comes. We
climb together. The sun breaks over the distant
mountains. Their craggy peaks are teeth biting it back. I
taste the energy on my tongue. Here is power. Here is truth. Here is
life. Away from the action. Away from the machines. Away from myself.
I kneel and touch
the stones. I am humbled by this
structure. Placed here stone by stone by my
ancestors. Perhaps not genetically my ancestors. But I am
the bearer of the torch of effort to improve my world, myself, and
help the people around me. The scent of fear is gone, but the clarity remains.
As do the steps.

RLS

SHE GOES SOFTLY

For Michelle

A vibrant life
Full of love and laughter
But time for thoughts
And what comes after

A life cut short
Too soon to die
So much to do
Your soul wants to cry

Things left unfinished
Loose ends untied
Places to go
Adventures untried

The world around
Careens on its way
But she goes softly
To a bright new day

CAS

JUST FOR FUN

THE SPIDERS' TEA PARTY

Mr. and Mrs. Spider sent out invitations

to all of the other bugs.

Please, come to our tea party

We have tea cups and mugs.

When the bugs showed up

The spiders welcomed them in

past one of the curtains,

shining in the dim.

SMMS

CHRISTMAS

Jingle go the bells

hanging o'er the door.

Bang! goes the door

as people go in and out.

Pitter-patter go the feet

climbing up and down the stairs.

Pling! sounds the piano

then we all join in song.

SMMS

BUILDING

There's a tiller in my kitchen
an icebox in the bath
a saw bench in the bedroom
and mortar in the path
We've been a while a'building
but I really shouldn't pout
We don't have to LIVE here
We're just campin' out!

TRAVELING

Here we go on a sunny day
over the hill and down
We'll go until we're far away
over the hill and down
We sing a cheerful little song
as we merrily ride along
That way the road is not as long
over the hill and down

CAS

96

GRACE, THE CLUBHOUSE MOUSE

One upon a time, in the Clubhouse near the spit
Little Gracie Churchmouse dearly loved to sit
hidden 'neath piano waiting for the choir
The joyful notes abounded and set her heart on fire
She sprinted out among the chairs
to hear the songs more clearly
But suddenly the music stopped –
they stared at her most queerly
With head hung low she scuttled back
to where they couldn't see
and when the choir began again,
she joined them cheerfully
The pianist lifts up her feet, sopranos start to giggle
whenever Gracie ventures forth with characteristic wiggle
From whence she came or how survives
is somewhat of a myst'ry
but Little Gracie's now a part of Purdy Clubhouse hist'ry

CAS

OWED TO A PROF

I live, I laugh, I love, thanks to my prof
He gives me food for thought
He gives me puns uncaught
Yes, I get quite a lot
       Thanks to my prof

I sing, I sleep, I move, thanks to my prof
He speaks in rhythmed tone
that soothes my mind alone
His actions I condone
       For he's my prof

I think, I work, I play, thanks to my prof
On this you can rely
I overwork, then sigh
For in the end . . . I die
       Thanks to my prof!

(A diligent Bact. 104 student, 1956)

CAS

GYPSY

Costumes and masks were not my things
nor draped with beads, bracelets, rings
But I'd be a gypsy to please my friend
with scarves and make-up without end
Gaudy colors for reluctant teen
made for fun that Halloween

CAS

PROB-A-BUB-AB-LY

For Sheridan

"Candy Mirandy," said Grandmother Sue
"I do need your help. I'm cooking a stew
Please get from the cellar a carrot or two
It will make dinner better for me and for you."

"Yes – no
       maybe so
               prob-a-bub-ab-ly"
said Candy Mirandy.
And she did.

"Candy Mirandy," said Grandfather Joe
"Look at my sock – there's a hole in the toe
Would you or could you fix it for me?
Then my toes will be cozy and warm as can be."

"Yes – no
       maybe so
               prob-a-bub-ab-ly"
said Candy Mirandy.
And she did.

"Candy Mirandy," said Great Aunt Louise
"I can't find my glasses – would you look for them,
please?
I can't see to read, I can't see to knit
And I must do something besides just sit."

"Yes – no
    maybe so
            prob-a-bub-ab-ly"
said Candy Mirandy.
And she did.

"Candy Mirandy," said Big Bully B
"I'd like you to go to the grocery with me
We'll take what we want and not pay a dime
I dare you to come – we'll have a great time."

"Oh, no!
    I'd never go
            Ab-so-loot-ally not!"
And she never did.

CAS

HILDA MATILDA

Hilda Matilda and Jennifer Jane
decided to go for a walk in the rain.
They put on their boots and mittens and caps
and bright yellow slickers with zippers and snaps.
They took their umbrellas and stepped out the door
splashed in the puddles and looked 'round for more
They stuck out their tongues and tasted the drops
then headed for home with jumps, skips and hops
It's fun to go out for a walk in the rain
said Hilda Matilda to Jennifer Jane.

Hilda Matilda and Jeremy Jake
wanted to mix up a big chocolate cake
They got out the eggs and the milk and the flour
put on their aprons and spent the next hour
measuring and mixing and having great fun
When Mother came in they agreed they were done
She wasn't too sure but put it to bake
and when it was done it looked like a cake.
A little lopsided but smelled very sweet
Even Mother agreed it was special to eat

Hilda Matilda and Micky Malone
were talking excitedly over the phone.
They whispered and giggled and laughed with delight
not once did they ever get into a fight
Hilda told stories and Micky told jokes
they related what happened to some silly folks
who always goofed up and never did well
They chittered and chattered for quite a long spell
Isn't it fun to talk on the phone
asked Hilda Matilda of Micky Malone.

Hilda Matilda and Michael McGee
pretended to sail on a ship out to sea
Hilda was Captain and Michael First Mate
The weather was sunny, the day was first rate
She steered their course while he read the map
He shinnied the mast to scout for mishap
He caught a salmon, she saw a whale
Adventures were many on that wondrous sail
Said Hilda Matilda to Michael McGee
Come again soon and go sailing with me

CAS

UNTITLED

When I was a little girl
with bright red hair
I climbed into a friendly whale
and went most everywhere

The windows in the house of whale
were made of jellyfish
And I used the oyster shell
To make a pretty dish

For lights I caught some fireflies
And cooked by electric eels
The myriad scallops and scallions
Were served for Sunday meals

We came upon a wondrous land
where streams ran soda pop
and chocolate mountains rose
with ice cream on the top

Candy trees grew in the dales
as thick as bamboo cane
Down fell drops of lemonade
instead of monsoon rain

Someday I'm going back again
Per chance I may take you
There's plenty there for both of us
and many others, too

So let us all be patient
till my whale comes back someday
when we shall quickly climb inside
and sail for old Cathay

JMO

BIOGRAPHIES

Colleen Slater wrote her first poem at age six. She is a local newspaper columnist who writes essays, articles, poetry and short fiction. Her work has appeared in anthologies, local and national magazines and online. She proofreads and edits special interest sections of a local monthly newspaper. As a member of the Northwest Independent Editors' Guild, she edits book length works for area writers. Her first published book is a local history, *The Key Peninsula.* She enjoys music, gardening, traveling, genealogy, and spending time with family and friends. www.colleenaslater.com; caoslats@gmail.com

James McCourt O'Hara, born and raised in Ayrshire, Scotland, came to U.S. in 1930 to make his fortune. He loved words and read dictionaries for fun, learning and using words new to him. He loved music, sang and danced at any opportunity. He had many jobs over the years, including logging in Washington state. His favorites were landscaping and bartending. A tablet of some kind was a close companion, where he noted phrases he liked, started stories, and composed a few poems. He entertained his children with songs and stories, some made up on the spot.

Robert L. Slater is a teacher/writer living in Bellingham, Washington. His stories and poetry have appeared in Story House, Continuum, SBD, Jackhammer, Goblin Muse, Martian Wave and on PBS in Earthscape. He has a should've-been-a doctorate B.A. in Theatre/Education, Spanish and History minors and M.A. in Educational Technology. He plays guitar, acts/directs in the Skagit River Shakespeare Festival, brews beer and mead, cooks, reads, practices Taekwon Do, writes plays, songs, and sings. He has six children, ages 7 to 25 years. His motto is Robert Heinlein's "Specialization is for Insects." www.robslater.com; rob@robslater.com

105

Sheridan M. Musick Slater graduated from Chugiak High School with honors in 2009. She's currently attending Western Washington University and pursuing a degree in everything. She's an active board member of Shakespeare NorthWest, a non-profit organization, and enjoys debating with the WWU debate team. In her spare time, when she has any, she enjoys reading books, swing dancing, reading The Economist, wandering beaches, watching movies, baking, acting, reading more books, singing, and playing Frisbee.

Ian R. Q. Slater is in eighth grade at Shuksan Middle School where he plays classical cello. He was one of a handful of seventh and eighth graders selected from Bellingham, and across the state for Washington Junior All-State. He also auditioned this past summer for a music camp called Marrowstone, and was accepted. He regularly participates in North Sound Youth Symphony at WWU. He has background as a thespian, appearing in plays with Shakespeare Northwest, the Bellingham Theater Guild, and a few other companies. His other interests include academics, reading, as well as writing, and a few sports.

Sarah Slater is currently a senior at Insight School of Washington, due to graduate in June 2011. She actively volunteers at Cascades Camp and Conference Center, a local Covenant camp, and attends horsemanship lessons monthly. She sings regularly on the worship team at Grace Covenant Church of Bremerton. Aside from drawing, in her spare time she enjoys reading, horse-back riding, swing dancing, playing video games, watching anything Sci-Fi, hanging out with friends, and listening to music.